EASTER

BY GAIL GIBBONS

HOLIDAY HOUSE · NEW YORK

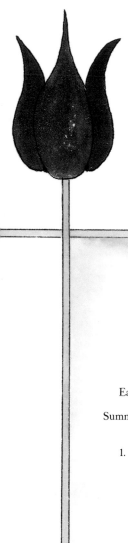

To my mother, GRACE ORTMANN

Copyright © 1989 by Gail Gibbons
All rights reserved
Printed in the United States of America

Library of Congress Cataloging-in-Publication Data

Gibbons, Gail.
Easter / written and illustrated by Gail Gibbons. — 1st ed.
p. cm.
Summary: Examines the background, significance, symbols, and
traditions of Easter.
ISBN 0-8234-0737-3
1. Easter—Juvenile literature.   [1. Easter.]   I. Title.
GT4935.G49 1989
394.2'68283—dc19   88-23292   CIP   AC

IBSN 0-8234-0737-3
ISBN 0-8234-0866-3 (pbk.)

Easter Sunday is in the spring.

Many years ago, baby Jesus was born. Some people believed He was the Son of God.

When He was ready, He began preaching and teaching. Soon
He had twelve followers called disciples. In the Bible
it is told that He performed many miracles.

More and more came to listen to Him. They found new
hope and strength from the words He spoke. Some of them
began to say He was the King they had been waiting for.

One day Jesus, a Jew, went to a city called Jerusalem with His disciples to celebrate Passover, the spring festival of the Jews.

 He rode into Jerusalem on the back of a donkey. Crowds gathered, spreading palm branches on the ground before Him. They waved palm branches and cheered, "Blessed is the King of Israel!"

Jesus ate the Passover meal with His twelve disciples.
He said He would be betrayed by one of them and would
die. They shared bread and wine. This meal is called
the Last Supper.

Afterward, the disciples followed Jesus to a garden,
where He went to pray. Jesus had enemies. One of His
disciples, Judas, told them where Jesus could be found.
The enemies seized Him, and the other disciples ran away.

Other enemies told Pontius Pilate, the governor of
Jerusalem, that Jesus was becoming too powerful. These
enemies accused Him of breaking laws and of claiming
to be God. They wanted Him put to death. "Crucify Him!"
some of them shouted. Pilate ordered that Jesus be
put to death.

Jesus was taken to a hill and nailed to a cross. There He died. He was taken down and carried away.

The body of Jesus was placed in a tomb. A huge stone was rolled in front of it.

On the third day after He had died, the stone was found rolled away and the tomb was empty. His followers remembered Jesus telling them that He would rise from the dead.

Jesus appeared several times to His followers during the forty days after His death. Then He ascended into heaven. The death of Jesus on the cross and the miracle of His rising from the dead are the heart of the Easter story.

Many Christians go to church to celebrate Easter Sunday.
Often candles are lit to remind people that after darkness
comes light, and after death comes new life.

There are Easter lilies and other spring flowers. They are symbols of new life and hope.

The word Easter comes from the word Eostre, the goddess of spring. Before the time Jesus lived, there were festivals thanking the gods for spring.

The egg is a symbol of new life. For thousands of years it was the custom to give eggs as gifts at spring festivals.

As part of the Easter celebration, some eggs are dyed with beautiful colors.

Some eggs are painted. Others are decorated.

There are Easter egg hunts. Eggs are hidden, and everyone rushes around to see who can find the most.

Each Easter a famous egg-rolling contest is held at the
White House where the president of the United States lives.

Easter eggs are placed in beautiful Easter baskets with candy and other treats.

Many children believe that the Easter bunny brings them their
Easter eggs. This legend began many years ago. There was a
story about a woman who dyed eggs for her children at
Easter. She hid them in a nest. When the children found
the nest, a big rabbit hopped away. They thought the
rabbit brought the eggs, and the story spread.

Families and friends get together for Easter. There may be an Easter ham, or lamb with mint sauce.

There are Easter parades. Some people dress up in new spring clothes and wear Easter bonnets.

Easter is a religious holiday and much more.

It is also a time of hope and joy.

EASTER HOLY DAYS

Lent is the forty days before Easter Sunday. It reminds us of the forty days Jesus spent praying in the wilderness before He went out to preach His message. For some, Lent is a time for prayer and sacrifice.

Ash Wednesday is the first day of Lent. In church, some Christians have a cross marked on their foreheads with ashes. It symbolizes their mortality.

Holy Week is the last week of Lent.

Palm Sunday is the first day of Holy Week. It reminds us of the ride Jesus took on a donkey into Jerusalem, when people waved palm branches.

Holy Thursday is celebrated in memory of the Last Supper, Jesus' last meal with His disciples.

Good Friday is in memory of Jesus dying on the cross. His death is called the Crucifixion.

Easter Sunday is the celebration of Jesus rising from death. His rising is called the Resurrection. The palms in the churches stand for peace, and the Easter lilies are symbols of new life and hope.